About the Author

Ch Woods works part time as a GP in Lancashire and tries to
bal e medicine, family and writing. His poetry has appeared in
nu rous magazines and newspapers including the *British Medical
Jo* *l, The Guardian, The Independent, Poetry Review, PN Review,
Th* *pectator* and *The Times Literary Supplement*. His work has been
br ast on BBC Radio and Channel 4 Television (*Rhyme and
R* and *Six Experiments that Changed the World*). He has been a
pri vinner in many poetry competitions, won the Peterloo and
be competition judge. His poetry has appeared in anthologies
in UK and America. This is his second collection.

First published in Great Britain in 2008 by Comma Press
3rd Floor, 24 Lever Street, Manchester M1 1DW
www.commapress.co.uk

A CIP catalogue record of this book is available from the British Library

ISBN: 1-905583-15-X
EAN: 978-1-905583-15-7

The publishers gratefully acknowledge assistance from the Arts Council England
North West, as well as the support of Literature Northwest:
www.literaturenorthwest.co.uk

literature**north**west

Set in Bembo by XL Publishing Services, Tiverton
Printed and bound in England by SRP Ltd, Exeter.

dangerous driving

CHRIS WOODS

ACKNOWLEDGEMENTS

Acknowledgements are due to the editors of the following publications, where some of these poems have previously appeared: *Acumen*, *The Independent*, *Iron*, the Lancaster LitFest Poetry Competition anthologies, *The Journal of Medical Ethics*, *Orbis*, *The Journal of Palliative Care*, *PN Review*, *Poetry Review*, *Scratch*, *The Spectator*, *Staple* and *The Journal of the Society of Medical Writers*. Several of the poems have been prizewinners in competitions and some broadcast on BBC Radio.

'Consultation' is an Arts Council commission for Poems for the Waiting Room. 'Images of War' and 'The Alzheimer Sea' have been adapted into short films by Scott Davenport and Fiona Collins.

The author would like to thank the members of Off the Page and his poetry friends in Manchester and London for their advice and support.

BY THE SAME AUTHOR

Recovery, published by Enitharmon, 1993.

To Brenda, Katy, Emma and our dog, Ben

CONTENTS

The Pool   1
On the Move   2
An English Holiday   3
Driving Back   4
Seaham Harbour   5
Radio Three   6
Knocking Through   7
Feverish   8
The Alzheimer Sea   9
Tonic   10
Consultation   11
Breathalysed   12
Dangerous Driving   13
Break In   14
The Illuminations   15
The London Classical Players Performing On Period
      Instruments   16
Black Hole   17
Bathyscaphe   18
Monster   19
Not Talking   20
Blue and Black   21
On Scout Moor   22
Farmhouse   23
The Colne Royal Morris Men Dancing at Ramsbottom
      Station   24
North West Water Comes to Holcombe Old Road   25
Pumpkin Lantern   26
Winter Lamp   27
Loggerhead Turtles   28

Diving	29
Light Out	30
First Thing	31
Fog	32
Escape	33
Hut	34
Racing Time	35
Good Fences Make Good Neighbours	36
By the Pool	37
Musée Picasso	38
Elements of Bargemon	39
Seasons	40
Letting Go	41
Time Piece	42
7am	43
Motorway Madness	44
Turning Light	45
A Way Through	46
The Library	47
Video Kid	48
Film, Tape and Chromosomes	49
Images of War	50
War Poet	51
November 11th	52
Going Back	53
Remembrance	54
Swimming at Mangen	55
Postcards from Greece	56
Sweden	58
Autumn Lamp	59
White Walk	60
A Christmas Story	61
The Lawn is Green	62

The Pool

is at the centre of the complex, cool blue
at the centre of our lives, as we stretch towards it
and watch the light working on the water.
The children keep returning, to look at themselves,
to leap into their centre and find refreshment there
or a rhinoceros beetle that tired of the concrete
coast of the pool like Majorca, threw itself in.

I wake up after two bottles of wine the night before,
my brain sunburned. Snakes of light move
across the bottom of the pool. Light loops through
the weave of water. The crickets noisy like water
through taps. White chairs sit round the pool
waiting for ideas to happen. Shadows mark out the light.
The children like purposeful porpoises.

I want to slow the days down, to move through them
as slowly as through the pool. Tap water tastes like sea.
No wonder everyone drinks lager here.
Bleary-eyed Balearics. A mesh of light protects the pool.
Veins of light through the pool's blue body. Sunflowers
turn their polyunsaturated faces to the sun, as we do.
Conversation sways like palm trees.

Ant bites like mountains, go down slowly like memories
of work. A nasty taste in the mouth and an overpriced
underwater salad at Valdermosa. Chopin was here
and George Sand. I really ought to write about that.
So I don't. The pool like a big blue bouncy castle,
the children jump up and down, up to their necks in fun,
or swim through the pool like the light.

On The Move

We are packed together
like the contents of a suitcase.
We cannot move.
We have to move
to another house.

We haven't enough rooms.
We haven't enough room
to swing a Katy,
who offers me a house
from her Early Learning Centre Liftout Puzzle Board,
as well as her Wendy House;
detached, in need of little upkeep,
in need of little people.

We are packed together
like the contents of a suitcase,
ready to go,
ready to be picked up,
in need of a holiday.

There will be room on the beach,
a living room,
a sheepskin rug of surf
in front of a Living Flame sunset,
quiet pictures,
flying seagulls hanging against the green wall
of a cliff

and Katy will build us a castle.

An English Holiday

Rain
pouring cold water on everything,
the holiday shrinking
to a room and a television
where sport takes place
in perfect weather.

An aluminium sky,
a crinkle cut beach,
a murderous wind
breaking the backs of the waves,
grinding them into the sand.

A washing up bottle,
washed up on the beach,
oil instead of shadows
clinging to our feet,
seagulls circling like vultures
over the holiday makers.

Then the sun coming out
and the people coming out,
drawn from their boxes
like iron filings,
arranging themselves on the beach
in rows,

or racing into the surf,
renewing their friendship with the waves
and the sea roaring back its greeting,
lifting them up,
slapping them on the back,
toasting them
with froth and liquid light.

Driving Back

We begin our journey at the end
of a bovine tailback,
cows jam the road ahead,
cover catseyes with cowpats.

A car starts up with the rattle
of a collecting box,
another leaves a smoky signature
along the dotted white line.

The kids are feverish.
The temperature is rising.
We wind down with the windows
as rain pockmarks the windscreen.

Only the radio stops talking
as we go under bridges.
Black tar clots inside my head.
I have white dots in front of my eyes.

Then sun sets a diamond on each car
and we wind down again,
steer our treasures
past caravans of caravans.

Late. A dead sandbag beside the road,
a motorbike roaring off
into a black leather night
studded with neon lights and stars.

The chips are down now.
Can we make Kan's Takeaway in time
to wrap up the day in newspapers
we haven't read for two weeks.

Seaham Harbour

for my father

The sea writes history here,
prints waves on the beach,
leaves its mark on the cliff,
its signature on the stone.

Here is the pull of the tide,
the incessant tug of memory
and meaning, as the sea takes
the sand and time away.

The tide is full and running,
as a boy sprints the length
of the harbour wall and stops,
to listen to the waves.

Soon he skims stones
across the surface of the sea
and sinks into thought.
His hands bridge his eyes.

He could skip to the horizon:
The future lies before him.
I stand looking at the past,
held by the harbour's embrace.

Radio Three

is surrounded by silence,
tune in and there is silence
at the end of each sound,
silence amplified by announcers
staying quiet until the echo
of sound has settled inside us.

Open your doors and your ears,
enter the studio of your car,
sit down in front of the music
and let your ears take it in.
Record music deep inside,
play it back and sing out loud.

I sang out, as interference
scurried to the edge of sound
to gnaw at the programmes.
I sang out, as hills altered sound
and I drove into a valley
where mist clung to music.

I hung on to the old radio
until the medium wave broke up,
exploded in a surf of static
and I nearly went under.
Now the new dials shine out
like lighthouses amid darkness.

Knocking Through

Conception occurs then development,
the skeleton is articulated,
the circulation joined up.

The house wakes to its new self,
yellow paint on brown plaster
like a sunrise lighting up Holcombe Hill.

This baby stirs under its duvet
of fibre glass. We wrestle
with responsibility, but it's too late.

We worry about water breaking in,
yet install more. We bother with burglar
alarms, but relish the remoteness.

The family is closer, yet further apart.
Exterior is the same, but interior
has been subject to deep analysis –

dreams, the strangeness of architraves.
We take shape inside this cocoon.
We ask old stone for new direction.

Feverish

Bright yellow phlegm;
such colour, such a source.
A fug in the car.
The windscreen perspiring.
Coughing.
Wipers taking drops of rain away.
Don't turn on the fan
or you'll suck in exhaust.

Tuned to the frequency of paracetamol,
amoxicillin
flowing down wires.
Talking like a robot;
heavy lipped and limbed.
A metallic taste in the mouth,
the smell of ozone in the nostrils.
Shorted.

Ears full of sea
and noises like lorries
or the touch on a record stylus.
Eyes full of grit and rain
and road.
Dazed, but seeing no stars
just a world
through cling film.

The Alzheimer Sea

Its motion
erodes memory, drags it
into the ocean.

Eyes brim full
as seas roar through
caves of skull.

The restless flood
casts up broken words
as driftwood.

A strange light
fills a sunken world
each night.

The sea seeks
the land, flows across
cracked cheeks.

No sleep.
just movements of tides,
life-times deep.

Tonic

The patient smokes fifty a day in a creaky-chested house
full of smoke. The doctor listens to Schubert in the car.
Honeyed sound and sputum, sublime and ridiculous.

Everything is back to front like the advert on the lorry
that has to be read through a rear view mirror.
Suddenly, Beethoven, in the midst of all this worry,

and sluggish feet begin to tap and the heart to pound.
Music like this lifts the cataracts from inward vision,
syringes wax from the ears with a jet of sound.

Music like this performs heart surgery and the pain
in the chest, the angina of the day, just goes.
Blood flows with the melody, circulates like life again.

Alternative medicine for the doctor when desired.
Handel is holistic, a tonic for mind, body and spirit,
to be taken through the ears as frequently as required.

Consultation

He doesn't look too good,
suit not as snappy.
His tie's a bit frayed.
He doesn't look happy.

Domestic difficulties,
staff shortages, cuts?
In the driving seat
no longer. Driven nuts.

He doesn't look too hot.
Has he been up all night?
I'll be supportive –
"Doc. Are you all right?"

Breathalysed

He slips out behind me, a shark
nosing out into Bridge Street behind his prey.
I'm drowning in waves of blue light.
Those blinking lights play

with me and over me. I pull in.
He pulls out his notebook. His lights
are working, mine are not.
He has so many reds, whites

and blues, all flashing patriotically.
Perhaps he could lend me one?
"You have committed a moving traffic offence, sir.
Can you step into my car, so I can take some

particulars?" I have been in a poetry pub
and downed a pint of lager.
Smoke clings to me like a wreath.
"I can smell alcohol on your breath, sir.

Can you blow into this, sir?"
He offers me the pipe of the machine,
invites me to blow my life away.
The smoke filled room, this spectral scene

haunt these moments of freedom.
He takes my name, rank and surreal number,
steals my good night
and waits forever. "You are under

the limit, sir. But don't drink any more."
I've had enough. Mobile
at last, I can breathe again. He was OK
apart from his arresting smile.

Dangerous Driving

A trapeze moon above a net
of light, street lamps in the valley
trapping the darkness.

Driving along, trying to feel safe,
only looking back in the mirror,
then seeing the flashing lights.

A quick slow, thinking of police,
but it's only cars going over bumps,
rearranging their photons.

In a jam, thoughts nose to tail,
red-eyed brake lights, fans coming on,
cooling off the choleric cars.

Wanting to be receptive to the night,
tuning in to city-centre static,
flicking through wavelengths like ideas.

Later, driving along the motorway –
Has someone stretched a wire across?
The horizon cuts me in two.

The night goes on around me,
there is nothing there and Radio One.
Feeling strung up like the moon.

Break In

The first sign is no window
and nothing else.
The car is still there and the radio.

Then I find the half-charlie,
the half brick on the back seat
sitting on its cushion of glass.

Rain pours in,
wind rushes in to fill the vacuum
left by my old jacket.

The alarm comes back to me,
it was a memory even then,
distant, barely recognised.

I battle with bin liners,
try to cover up the lack of glass.
The wind wraps itself up.

I wish weather on the jerk
who nicked my jacket,
it lets in water like my window.

The Illuminations

Tasty, but a little bit tacky now –
rock, candy floss, toffee apples,
plastic buttocks and a doughnut man
printing zero after zero.

Children create their own magic,
wave wands of light
bought from flashy conjurors
who make money disappear.

Grown-ups walk the length of the lights
and beyond into darkness,
then try to find a way back
and a seat on the tram.

They climb on, empty the night,
and find a cheeky-chappie conductor
to brighten things up.
Feet glow.

Mums and dads, wrapped up
like their fish and chips,
glance at lights that once upon a time
burned brightly inside them.

The London Classical Players Performing On Period Instruments

for Roger Norrington

Strands of cotton hang
from the mouthpieces
of bassoon and oboe.

Patches of glue shine
as clarinet and violin
catch the studio lights.

The whole has the feel
of a balsawood plane
lovingly kitted together,

light, effortlessly fast,
so easy in its flight
as music rushes past.

Soaring on thermals
of sound to the heights,
I can hear for miles.

Black Hole

You turn all the lights off
but never sleep,
pace round the edge of yourself,
never communicate.
A million dark years distant,
you suck in light like spaghetti.

You got too big for yourself
and collapsed,
but ferocious energy remained
and now you're back, muscling in
carving out your own space
and time.

You smash up your neighbourhood,
pull the light off stars.
Masked,
you are far outside our laws,
giving nothing away,
stealing everything from everything.

Bathyscaphe*

A furrowed seabed
then a deeper frown;
the Mariana Trench
and going down.

At the bottom,
sweat and pressure,
messages back to ship
crackle and blur.

Dark fashions dark,
things look in and leer,
only darkness makes sense
down here.

Wanting to stay,
to pull the lever back,
to let darkness in,
then pulling back

and rising up,
having to learn
how far to go
in order to return.

Out of darkness,
the first hint of blue,
fingers of sunlight,
then you.

* In 1960 the bathyscaphe *Trieste* reached the sea bed in the Mariana
Trench near the Pacific island of Guam. At a depth of 35,813 ft (10.92
km), this is the deepest part of the world's oceans.

Monster

Lightning jolts me to life,
a rivet through my neck
holds on another's head.
I wear deadmen's shoes,
an overcoat from another life
and people keep walking away.

In Frankenstein's library
all I want to do
is crawl under the table,
stack books around me,
wall myself in with words,
and seal myself inside myself.

Perhaps my own writing
is only talking about all this,
trying to understand.
Perhaps this existence
is necessary to dam up words
then release them with force.

On November the Fifth
there is no bonfire
inside my head, no sparks
or rockets of emotion.
I want to set fire
to the darkness inside me,

and let flames lick my lips.
I am tired of the shadows,
but all I can ever do
is write about them,
created never to be whole,
a monster of spare parts.

Not Talking

Bury the hatchet, but not in him.
Uncurl the fist and shake hands.

Find common ground on the road
and walk towards him, not away.

We banged together at random,
mere Brownian movement,

now there's a grudge like icebergs
grinding together, cold shouldering.

Backs turn as we go inside
ourselves and slam the door.

Stop this pacing up and down
inside your head and walk round,

invite him to a get together
even though he won't come.

Should have had it out with him.
Should have had it out on the road.

Difficult to clear the air
now leaves burn and smoke invades.

Blue and Black

Mouth stopped up.
Choking on darkness
too profound
to express.

Hurt, lettered through
bitter rock.
Hit,
it crazes with shock.

On this planet,
no sun's ray
reaches the dark side.
Face turned away.

Mechanical,
only skeleton.
The warm flesh
has gone.

No music,
the sound is sore,
a reminder of that
which is no more.

Inside a shell,
no sight no sound.
Is there grit
to coalesce around?

On Scout Moor

a skylark sings
through vast blue speakers.
Hills curve, wings
lift and the moor breathes in,
breathes out blue.
Cotton grass cleans the CD
of the sky, new
music spins round Knowl Hill;
pure curlew.

The air is wine-cellar cool
in the hill's
shadow. A stream flows
over grass, fills
with light, spins visions
of moorland along
its length; whirlpools of sky
that belong
here, sacred in a throat
full of birdsong.

Farmhouse

Pant Glas

Flakes of whitewash settle
on rotting carpets, black
earth and shadows edge rooms
with no corners, a sack
over a doorway admits the sun,
dust rises up to reveal
the rays, walls and ceilings
are moss, floors have the feel
of outside where worms come
to weave and wait for rain.
This house is its own compost;
all earth comes back again.
There is change but no movement
now, as new life shrouds
rotting timber and green light
grows. And then clouds
of wallpaper separate and drift,
black fungus scribbles
on walls that lean in to listen
to themselves, moisture dribbles
into the warm open earth,
roots tangle and embrace.
Here is the deep smell of soil
and alteration, an empty place
full of ferns and wild flowers
where sunlight tends the surface.

The Colne Royal Morris Men Dancing at
Ramsbottom Station
for David Swithenbank

Blossoming hats in bunches
nodding with weight and music,
russet faces, catkin beards
and a sash as blue as the sky.

Summer timed with clicking clogs,
stone flags patterning the dance,
rectangular sound, simply tuneful,
the sun pushing forward to watch.

The train puffing out its rhythm,
whistling to change direction,
crossing and recrossing on lines
then moving off into the morning.

Men and men and trees
reaching up towards the light,
swaying to the pulse of the wind,
the clarinet and accordion,

then linking up like carriages,
pulling away along the pavement
to raise pints of beer to sunlight
and a day heady with fun.

North West Water Comes to Holcombe Old Road

The men come early,
pick out the secrets of the road,
dissect down to clotted pipes
to graft in the new.

Water leaps in the air,
escapes from its dungeon
deep underground,
where it hears no wind
only the rush of itself.

Men sound the silence,
knee deep in holes full of water,
beneath a sky full of water
emptying its contents
down the slopes of the hill
and the glistening waterproofs.

Lengths of new pipe
swallow up the emptiness,
slither over cobbles,
threading themselves through the earth,
charmed by the men
and the fluted wind.

Yellow lamps flash like lighthouses,
stand against the darkness
that washes across the road.
Mechanical diggers slumber now,
scoops full of shadow.
Compressors squeeze the silence no longer.

The men depart,
leave the day buried deep in the road.

Pumpkin Lantern

Eyes gouged out
and the brain,
yet lit from within,
orange light
for orange flesh.

A luminous grin,
unaccommodated
pumpkin man,
light moving
behind your eyes.

At midnight
your inner flame
burns brightly.
You have changed
into yourself.

Winter Lamp

A sycamore
against a dark sky,

a tinsel of stars
between branches.

The tree's scent
is a surprise,

a seasonal gift
out of season.

A streetlamp
lights the tree,

as I walk through
levelling snow.

All is different
but the same

in this winter
white and innocent.

Loggerhead Turtles

The neon strip of the coast is turned off
and bathers come out of the sea at night.

They carry their progeny to the beach
and bed them deep under sun loungers.

The children grow beneath waves
of sand and hatch in the deepest night,

then race beneath a lunar floodlight
to the mountainous applause of seas.

Baby turtles flow across sand to the surf,
a living tide pulled by the moon at night.

They must avoid the bright lights of hotels
or they will be forever led astray.

No one helps. Mum has gone and Dad
just hangs around on the corner of a reef,

so the youngsters back-pack new shells
and life is a beach to get off fast.

Diving

The heavyweight belt and metal tank
on my back cannot stop me and all is gone

to floating in weightless worlds down here.
No pain now only pressure to be got rid of.

Will ears pop or explode? I hold my nose
and blow and suddenly I hear crackles

as I tune-in to a different wavelength –
buoyed up and the sea flowing through me,

I'm moving outwards along veins of light.
There is blue inside and out and no weight

as fish swim past, schools of rainbows
oblivious to bubbles that thunder upwards.

And light is lightning caught in crystal
as I look up to a swirling ceiling of light,

to chandeliers that are constantly moving,
to chandeliers and no ceiling, only light.

Light Out

The world is somewhere else
in this painful fog.
He cannot find himself

or unravel the mysteries
of a day, mummified
in sad-cloth wrap around.

There is no blue sky,
the sun shines the other way.
He wakes to a nightmare,

cannot dream anymore.
The dawn chorus
greets everyone else's day.

No corner to curl up in,
no hearth or firelight,
thoughts flicker and go out.

First Thing

He wakes early
and pushes back blankets
before night covers him again.

He stumbles along
to the bathroom,
tries to wash shadows away.

Downstairs, in the silence
before the house wakes,
he sits down,

turns on the lamp
and feels safe
within its tent of light.

He begins to write
and black ink is shadow
released across the page.

Fog

He walks towards it
and away. It's all the same.
Nobody sees him.

He can find no one
to help. Sound has gone
and there is no smell.

Fog stops him up.
He breathes it in and out,
making it himself.

In this house of fog,
the walls are shadows
but there is no sun.

In this cold enclosure
all he knows is the ground
he stands on.

Escape

No longer locked in place
by a seat belt life,
where flailing arms

and nodding heads are allowed
but no walking away.
He faces the sun now,

the shadows are behind him.
He can take off his cares
and float, buoyed up

in clear, uncomplicated water.
He removes his tie
and the rash round his neck.

He forgets to wind up his watch
and the hairs on his wrist.
Time hurts no longer.

Hut

Breathe space and woodscent,
count the emptiness
in and out.

Held by walls
and light through windows
and darkness and stars and mist only.

Free to leave and come back.
Free to laugh –
tongue in cheek and groove.

He fits together now,
joins up
as simply as the hut itself.

Safe inside and alone.
Not trying to be something else.
Not trying to be a hut and a half.

Racing Time
for Ron Heaton

He elbows the cold morning aside,
a string vest, seventy years and legs
bowed like the trees but just as sturdy.

Shorts billowing like the clouds,
chin inclined to the hill, he will eat up
the distance, have the hill for breakfast.

The starting gun was the crack of knees
first thing then a stretch into the morning,
a dawn chorus of approval everywhere.

The breeze in the sails of his shorts,
as he battles up the waves of the hill,
the effort breaking on his sheer face.

He stumbles, but does not give way
fights back, tramples the hill under foot
and the hill pushes back with strength.

His arms pump, pistons punch the air,
pummel the morning, bare knuckles,
knobbly knees in the groin of the hill.

Because it is there, because he is there,
because he will never hang up his heart,
he plants the flag of himself on the top.

Good Fences Make Good Neighbours

Feuding over fences,
words exploding
then the fall out,
with a sick feeling left behind.
Only frost and frozen glances

until now and snow
and trying to dig ourselves out,
wearing breath like scarves.
We must warm
towards each other,

rise above this frozen waste
of time,
not just speak hot air.
We must brave the snowfields
where sound is put down

and movement restricted.
We must escape
from this totalitarian state
of ice
and drink the melt water.

By the Pool

I feel light first thing and surprise,
normally my dark time with days.

A few moments alone here
by clear water edged with old stone

that seems to be lit from within.
The heart floats upwards

through depths of sky to the sun.
Bare feet on dew on grass

in the morning sun when light
flames the surface of the pool.

Just to move through the water,
the ripples only and a direction

as I swim through a summer day;
still air and blue sky and pool sky,

as I push out into the morning
and the soft glide through.

Musée Picasso

Rustic white washed
bits of stone and space,

paintings hung on space
and space itself –

wallpaper surrounding
his ceramics of earth.

All this as we move
through light, windows

like works of art of blue
distance and the sea.

Walking through
deep light and space

with the children
who do not complain,

who walk happily with us
this day in Antibes.

Elements of Bargemon

Ants cross the table where I write.
Words, spindly like trails through ink,

join up the blue green distance
as sky and trees march to the sea.

Over the hill, people on the beach
colonise the coast; brown bellies,

earth not yet torched by forest fire,
and water that is fired by the sun.

Spray is light, water through pipes
and gutturals through throats –

lovely when it stops, but the lawn
needs water and the silence, noise.

Here are the simple things I need
and here is peace pumped through

blue pipes of sky, old passageways
of Bargemon, into the air around me.

Seasons
for my father

You throw green
and light in one.
Cut grass is fire
in the evening sun.
You wrestle me,
and grass clings,
the light holds
a blackbird sings.

Body-surfing;
waves climbing high,
peaks melting
into sky,
arms out in front,
flurries of spray,
avalanches of light
carrying us away.

Cricket
as the light goes,
the sun behind you.
With shadows
reaching out,
you touch the horizon,
then dazzle me
bowling the sun.

Frozen feet,
fingers not there,
snow and silence
everywhere.
You bring me back
on my sled,
then my fingers back
from the dead.

Letting Go

Don't pretend
you never loved.

Don't put her outside
and close the door.

Don't tear up her memory
and put it in the bin.

Don't push her away,
it hurt too much before.

Let the tears
of her flow out.

Let her flow out
as she flows through.

Let the wild animals go
to attack at will.

Let go of the bars
and climb out too.

Time Piece

Your face
reflects my face,
your hands

my mouth,
sometimes smiling
or downcast.

You present
a glassy stare
to the world,

precise,
regular in your habits,
predictable.

You must stop
going round
in circles.

Wind down,
smash the glass
and escape.

7am

dark morning,
car in the freezer
of last night,
toughened frost,
de-icer that won't,

hot water on door
held in permafrost,
tug on handle,
alarm going off

then deep inside
ignition,
then wipers
then bits of rubber
stuck to a screen,

ice on the inside
try to look forward,
ice on the mirror
do not look back.

Motorway Madness

A fogged mind
and no insight

into the mist.
He is deluded.

thinking nothing
lies in front.

Thoughts go
out of control,

crash together,
link up crazily

as metal
hooks onto metal.

Relationships
are misjudged.

He is too close
to the other

and rebuffed
badly dented,

he is driven
to destruction.

Turning Light

It isn't Coleridge evading the elements
by the wall at the top stile or talking to
the wind whining over a dictaphone,

altering sound, like tinnitus, to a sea
inside a skull. But he's at home with sea
and sea is at home inside that cave,

washing around the salt-scoured bone,
with the wind tumble-drying the whites.
He opens a door on scents of sunshine,

and wants to take a turn with the light,
as sun flickers on distant roofs and rain.
A tin foil mind and an edgy glittering sun

wrap themselves around the morning,
as he huddles around his dictaphone,
furtively lighting up a pack of ideas.

A Way Through

The news is so bad
even the broadcasters sound shaken.
The car radio picks up the noise
of the world crashing, the traffic jam of voices,
the cries for help.

A red light flares
through the misted windscreen:
a firework in September.
Reluctant to turn on headlights
in case Summer is startled
and runs off.

Yesterday with the kids,
high up on the climbing frame,
tuned to the frequency of butterflies.
And the roundabout
that kept turning, a memory
after we'd gone.

A dictaphone; a black box recording
of our flight over the Pennines.
A refusal to be overwhelmed;
a farm on the M62
forcing the motorway
to split round it.

The Library

Shut at seven.
Wind and rain.
Beer cans
in a doorway,
pushed about
or inert
like the lads.

Books closed.
Shutters down.
The lights off.

Locked out,
no chance
of coming in,
the lads read
the writing
on the wall –
"Fuck off Ken"

or drink beer
as night
consumes them.

Video Kid

Blank face,
switched off,
deaf
to the high-volume-
household.
My one sided chat
does not go
through her head,
pale eyes
for the screen only.

Programmed,
wanting nothing
except the tape
to play through her.
No friends.
The machine
plays with her
as life reels past
on fast forward.

Film, Tape and Chromosomes

Video tape slithers on its belly,
coils round the necks of the young
and takes their breath away,
coils round the minds of the young
as they smash the pensioner's skull.

The rule of law is bent
like an iron bar over the head.
Lives are edited and the bits
litter the floor as children in pieces
pick up smashed plates at home.

We watch ourselves on the news
passing bucks like batons
in a relay race, passing on genes
as race and tribe dominate
and we all go to war.

Crowds gather to watch serial killers
become celebrities on TV.
Film stars become serial killers
and wade to their ceremonies
through deep red carpets.

The TV set brims with blood
and there's added bone, to force
the imagination, as kids beam up
on satellite TV or watch Cyber Mutants
and parents smash up the Earth.

Images of War

pile up like dead bodies.
Torture victims cannot speak,
but wounds mouth the hurt.

Spindle arms and legs, figures
in a grotesque Lowry painting;
stick men, stone faces, broken bones.

Neighbours erect wire fences,
chatter with gunfire, clear the soil,
fertilise it with blood and bone.

Grey faces haunt the television screen
and my sleep. Their nightmare
is mine. Their silence cries out.

Prisoners are white flags of flesh.
Ribs line up like barbed wire.
I cannot escape.

Children lie side by side on marble slabs,
tucked up under white sheets.
Life is play, played with, destroyed.

Images snipe at me while I run
between thoughts, looking for shelter.
Anger pours from the wound.

War Poet

A scarred landscape, acne,
testosterone and blood,
periscopes and the whistle
to start the game in a field of mud.

The iambic tread of the blind, hands
to shoulders, strolling just strolling.
Bits of bodies, heads distant
from hearts like generals patrolling

the outposts of ego. He creates
images in the cave of his skull;
a place of sanctuary, where he
puts down fear, finds its full

range and waits for a dawn
full of darkness as the guns stop.
Very Light. Very God no more.
A piss before going over the top.

November 11th

A two minute silence
at Rossett Ghyll, remembering
gawky lads in shorts and boots

charging in steel hats. I climb
with their spirit to Angle Tarn.
Let us see the sights together.

The sheep, simple and benign,
open-faced like the fell itself.
Mountains and sky: electricity

through blue green wires.
At the summit, two lads
on mobile phones, "We're on

Scafell Pike. Yes. Scafell Pike.
See you in the pub at eight"
Let us walk the path together

to the Old Dungeon Ghyll Hotel.
Evening, mellow darkness,
then a pint of Old Peculier.

Going Back

I eat an orange on Helvellyn summit
and remember that sun, the race
down scree slopes, woodsmoke,

the clear icy tarn where I swam.
Now leaves lie under trees like light
and the sun is a bonfire on the horizon.

A beer garden at Sawrey, a packet
of crisps, leaves clicking down
through desiccated autumn fellows.

The peace of the fells, as pieces fall
into place, a patchwork of landscape,
the weave changing with weather.

I want to put on that rumpled coat
and walk round Grasmere again
as I did when I was alive to the place.

I want to dig down through strata,
radiocarbon date that other time
and find myself again in this earth.

Remembrance

A Dove Cottage dawn;
poppy light and postcards
to families telling of fells

the colour of Ordnance Survey.
I unpack my map and boots
and feet. Will knees pack up

or carry me to the summit?
A cool stream from the tarn,
an avalanche of sparkling air

washes the heaviness away.
I will climb Helvellyn for you
because you fought for here.

I want to climb for your lives
out of the shroud-mist below,
and find you on the summit

in the company of the poet
who once saw Great Gable
on fire in the evening light.

Swimming at Mangen

Sweden

So much sun, blue sky, green forest
and clear water pollinated with pine scent.
Pushing the shore away, pulling back distance,
swimming through summer out into the lake.

Sun sparking on water, sky rippling,
soft water circling as I go under,
breathing out bubbles that tingle my face,
lift my hair then rise up before I do.

A cool clean wind skimming the surface
as I go into and out of the light.
The sky is stitched seamlessly to the water
and I am hypnotised by the swing of the sun.

Moving together, moving so easily together,
simply sliding through water, held by beauty
that takes all heaviness away, opens up to me,
opens wide to take each thrust and dive.

Postcards from Greece

Stale air and smoke in the apartment
and someone else's cold.
We wake up clinging to spinning beds
as blinds shred the sunlight
onto the bedroom floor.
Outside, on the balcony,
the kids turn their chairs round
to view the wild landscape of their rooms.

We hire shade from Antonio Sunbeds
and feel flat as the sea this morning.
Only the para-glider takes off.
We swim inside ourselves,
stay within the shadow of the umbrella
and let the beach go on outside.
We move with the shade,
sun-dialled.

The rental car is a Ford Fiasco,
cracked windscreen, no shock absorbers.
We drive along the beaten up track,
unable to judge edges,
eyes like binoculars on the road ahead,
searching for potholes.
No time for the view.
Mirtos Bay, the most scenic tyre change.

An orbital Emma and Katy in the taverna.
They will not come down.
We found a locust on the beach,
blown across from Africa. We cannot eat.
A dead swordfish hangs by the door,

bleeding into a tin.
A trail of aftershave back home,
then hunt-the-mosquito before it dines.

Our usefulness as clients is over now.
We pile up outside with our suitcases
to soften in the sun.
The kids blur their sequence of playmates
as easily as the beach does waves.
We peel off our anxieties,
leave them in a heap on the sand
and go for one last swim.

Sweden

Suddenly finding them,
strawberries collecting around themselves,
red swollen fruit
bending the stalks downwards.

Pillows for light to lie on,
flecks of sunlight on skin
seeding into flesh,
glowing in the dark,
red lights
in the foggy green darkness.

Feeling their deliciousness
through a fur of fern,
swollen plump fruit
heart-shaped in half,
handfuls of summer and juice
pressed against lips and tongue.

Autumn Lamp

Darkness flows
with the stream.

Leaves murmur
near crisp water.

Lamps light
a corridor of road:

old stone cottages
dry stone walls

a cobbled floor,
a ceiling of trees

in sodium,
a yellow autumn:

cottages painted
in moonlight

windows glowing
with memories.

White Walk

Even with a boot full of water
it was a good day out.
I climbed to Harcles Hill,
but lost myself for a second
in a white out of memory.
Sun sparkled on snow
and on the stream,
as I walked on with water
that slowly warmed up.

Holcombe Moor under white,
a green frisbee under snow
and a whitish labrador
polar-bearing about,
hunting for a hole in the ice.
You could smell the snow
and cold and silence.
I waded through whiteness,
up to my knees in dazzle.

A Christmas Story

Kids tearing into presents,
pinching each other's favourite,
adding sauce to their meal
of gifts, making themselves sick
with laughter and chocolate
from tree and stocking.

Crackers, opening salvos
in the wars of the families.
People taken apart like turkey.
Yellow, orange and red hats
flame on heads, as candles
burn up and splutter.

A time to be got through.
A time for wrapping yourself up
in a tissue of red wine,
a string of quiet expletives
and giving yourself to yourself.
A time to escape.

Driving over the Pennines,
where yellow light ices
the motorway, and the frosted moor
gleams like Christmas cake.
Pushing the pause button
on the endless merriment tape.

The Lawn is Green

The sheds have been removed.
The operation is complete.
Turf covers the raw earth
and the graft seems to be taking.
It has not curled up or died
and is sprightly around the edges.

We are moving outside
for the summer, into the open air
extension at the side of the cottage,
with its new green carpet,
its sky blue ceiling
and a garden gate for a door.

The children lie on the lawn,
under the scent of grass
and doze, dreaming on green.
They grow simply and straight,
spring back after pressure
and welcome both sun and rain.

They develop green knees
and green fingers as they plunge
into this pool of grass.
Katy does a forward somersault
and Emma, the crawl,
elbowing the distance to one side.